Whispers Of My Soul

BY

Ayesha Ahmad

"Poetry is the whispered secret of the soul, a symphony of words that weaves emotions into eternity"

About The Author

Ayesha Ahmad (D/o Dr Mohammad Faizan Ahmad and Fatima) was born on 22 November 2010 and is a student of St. Mary's Senior Secondary School, Moradabad, Uttar Pradesh. Inspired by her grandfather Mr. Rashid Jamal Farooqui Rashid, (a well known urdu poet) and encouraged by her Parents and teachers **(Mrs. Anju Johri- hindi teacher and Sir Nikhil Charan, A well known Musician of the city),** Ayesha started writing poems at the age of 12. And her first poem was" **The Good Old Days**". She has already written more than 20 poems in 3 languages I.e English, Urdu and Hindi. Some of them are presented in this book.

Acknowledgment

The world is a better place to thanks people who wanna develop and lead others. Thus, I would like to Express my heartfelt gratitude to all those who supported me in the creation of my poetry book. At the top of the list, I would like to thanks my Grandparents who showered their blessings and prayers upon me, which kept me going. Then my father's uncle (or my grandfather again), ***Mr. Rashid Jamal Farooqui Rashid****, a great Urdu poet, and my only source of inspiration, who helped me a lot in the journey of writing. Then, my parents who dedicated their lives for me, just to keep me* up. My parents being teachers helped me develop the sense of discipline in writing.

Last, but not the least, my hindi teacher **Maam Anju Johri,** who is the only source of motivation in my school. She motivated a lot throughout the journey.

But, I would like to Express my most special thanks to, **Sir Nikhil Charan** (A well known Musician+ My music teacher). Sir, this book would not have been possible without you. I can't express in words, how you, as a brother and as a teacher, supported me, how you've helped me in my school and my writings.

Thank you so much sir, for finding out the capabilities in me. Your mentorship and support have been invaluable to me as I worked on this book.

At last, my dear Kith and kins, I am honored to have such inspiring and motivating individuals throughout my journey. I am forever grateful to you all. Thank You for being a part of this journey.

Preface

Welcome to **Whispers Of My Soul**, a collection of poems born from the depths of my soul. Within these pages, I invite you to embark on a journey through the ebbs and flows of life, love, and self-discovery.

These poems are fragments of my heart, woven together by threads of hope, longing, and resilience. They tell stories of joy and sorrow, of dreams and disappointments, and of the human spirit's capacity to persevere.

May these words resonate with you, console you, and inspire you to find beauty in the everyday moments. May they remind you that you are not alone in your struggles or your triumphs.

And most of all, may they awaken something within you - a spark of empathy, a whisper of courage, or a gentle nudge toward the beauty that surrounds us.

Ayesha Ahmad

Contents

☆ENGLISH☆

☆HINDI☆

Am Okay...

Am Okay

They made me heartless,
Ignoring the efforts that were tireless.
They used to tell me that,
I should never feel bad.
Well, as you speak every part,
It Badly pierces my heart.
To escape the season, I just read,
Deep down somewhere, my heart
bleed.
To make their worry fade away,
I just say, Am okay.
Not knowing the story behind,
Ignoring things as if blind.
They erased my way,
And yet I say, Am okay.
I can't feel the pain,
And I can't feel the world anymore.
I can't feel any loss or gain,
And I can't keep my tears anymore.
They made my smile fade away,
And yet I say, AM OKAY.

The
Scrambled
Poetry

A Scrambled Poetry

The moment she used to be free,

She would sit down under a tree.

Tears would roll down her cheek,

Saying things she couldn't speak.

With a painful heart,

She would say the things that made her a part.

A part of a place can't be explained,

A place, where the dreams were chained.

Sitting in a corner,

She would explain.

Explain to herself,

The unbearable pain.

This unbearable pain,

Was then explained to the rain.

Soothing was her voice,

But bad was her choice.

The smile was fake,

With a severe heartache.

Deep in her eyes,

You may see the tears.

The tears may tell you,

The pain she bears.

They roll down her cheek,

Saying things, she couldn't speak.

In The Middle of
a Crowd
To make you
Proud

In the Middle Of A Crowd

I forgot I had a family,
And I forgot I had friends.
I forgot I had a smile,
And I forgot I had trends.
Many things to leave,
And something to achieve.
In the middle of a crowd,
To make you proud.
I was left behind,
To be renewed and designed.
But dear mom and dad,
I was pretty bad.
I tried and Cried,
And yes I decide.
Am gonna work- Unidentified,
And will be qualified.
Someday,
With success in my hand,
I'll stand in the middle of a crowd,
To make you proud.

HAPPY
friendship
day

Friendship Day

Hello Bae,
Its friendship day.
A Wonderful day,
As we say.
Everything we own,
We always share.
All the time together we spare.
Together the Celebrations,
Caring for generations.
In this era of people so fake,
I met you, for some memories to make.
In every story,
You are my glory.
In every rhyme,
Or any crime Together we shine.
I love you from the bottom of my heart,
Thank you for being my life's most valuable part.

♡(For Aamna)♡

happy
birthday

A Birthday Poem

On this day,
I just wanna say.
Happiest Birthday,
In every way.
This day is new,
And belongs to you.
On this great day,
I pray for you.
And here we gather,
To celebrate together.
The day that just,
Belongs to you.
On your Birthday, I honor you,
For all the amazing things you do.
In your wisdom,
We find our way.
Its true that,
You make our day.
May this year be filled with delight,
As you make our future bright.

☆(For Brother's Birthday)☆

Butterfly

BUTTERFLY

Butterfly! Butterfly!
Flying in the coloured sky.
I gaze you as you fly away,
As You fly in my way.
In the fields as you go,
Feel the magic air that blow.
♡(For My Lil Sis)♡

MoM

Precious Pearl

You came in my life,
And made it well.
Your love is precious,
I can never sell.
It's a pleasure,
You are a treasure.
I love the way,
The way you talk,
The way you walk.
The way you look and smile at me,
If I would have ever to choose my life
It would be thee.
My life was in darkness,
You made it glow.
You made me cheer,
When I was at my low.
I love you from the bottom of my
heart,
Thank you for being my life's most
valuable part.

♡(For My Mother)♡

Grandfather...

My Grandfather

His heart is bright,
And shines with might.
He is lovely,
and give us light.
He is sympathetic,
His words are aesthetic.
He educated an early me,
The one I praise is only he.
For his long life I do pray,
In my life for the role he play.
from childhood till now,
he told me "how?".
Grandpa it's you,
the shining star.
I hope you know,
what you are,
two others and me.
May you be glee.
♡(For my grandfather)♡

Winter
COZY

Winter Breaks

Its Holiday,
Sharing, caring and a hobby day.
After a long tiring month,
Finally!! Its Winter Break.
To have some coffee and hot chocolate shake.
Its winter break,
A lots of memories,
Memories to make.
Not meant to study,
Parents aren't ready.
Every place to go,
And everyone to know.
Its winter break,
Memories to make.

♡Friends♡

FRIENDS

Hi girls,
Give a cheers.
Its caring day,
I mean, FriendShip day
As we say.
Everything we own,
We always share.
All the time,
Together we spare.
Together the Celebrations,
Caring for generations.
In every story,
You are my glory.
In every rhyme,
Or any crime
Together we shine.
You fought for me,
You care for me.
For all these things,
I thank thee.

A POEM FOR MY TEACHER

Has deep brown eyes,

And soothing voice.

Has specs on his nose,

And smells like rose.

With a recorder in his hands,

With confidence he stands.

As noticed, his favorite shirt is blue,

Or maybe not, as I've no clue.

He sits in the lab,

Resting on a chair back.

"Choir is mine!"- he says with proud,

He asks for our justice in the middle of a crowd.

He makes us smile,

With his huge candy pile.

His gesture is sweet,

And his writing- so neat.

Regrets, complains and anxiety he listens,

Then sits with us and gives us lessons.

He makes our day,

And for his long life

I do pray.

☆(For Sir Nikhil)☆

REVENGE

Swinging in the open air,
Nobody is here, nobody is there.
You sing upon a mystery,
Remembering the history.
You cry all days, All days and nights,
Fighting and getting rights.
Come on and get up bros,
Make up some fed up shows.
Lil bit closer , lil bit near,
Let them have a little bit fear.
Let them know,
And
Let them show.
The people we are,
Known afar.

My Younger Sibling

You make me laugh,
And you make me cry.
You make my eyes go wet,
And you make them dry.
My love for you is undefined,
And a brother like you is impossible to find.

♡(For my dearest and loveliest brother AFFAN)♡

Happy
रक्षा बंधन

Raksha Bandhan

Dekho aaya raksha Bandhan,

Bhai behen k pyaar ka Bandhan.

Rakhi ki tum aaj nibhaana,

Bhaiya mera saath nibhaanaa.

Achcha bhaiyya ek hi hai,

Sacha bhaiyya ek hi hai.

Dekho rakhi bandh rahi hu,

Tumko sang mai bandh rahi hu.

Rishta kayi hai is duniya mai,

Per ye rishta kuch khaas hai.

Rakhi k dhagon sang bandhta hathon per vishwas hai.

Bhai ki kalayi pr behen ka pyaar,

mubarak ho aapko Rakhi ka tyohar.

Mai likhti hun

LIKHTI HUN

Mai likhti hun, Mai likhti hun.
Jo bol nahi sakte ,
Mai unki boli likhti hun.
Chidiyon ki chehchahaat likhti hun,
Pedon ki sarsarahat likht hun...
Mai likhti hun.
Jo kaha nahi jaata mujhse,
Mai Usko ispr likhti hun.
Mai likhti hun...
Kyunki,
Baaten sabki sehti hu.
Maimkuch baaton ko likhti hun,
Mai kuch raaton ko likhti hun.
Mai likhti hun...
Kyunki,
Mai likh sakti hun.
Mai har chahat ko likhti hun,
Mai har aahat ko likhti hun.
Mai likhti hun...
Kyunki,
Mai likh sakti hu.

Mai Likhta Raha

Gul murjha gaye
Abr barasta raha.
Ashq yeh shabnam bane,
Mai tarasta raha.
Ek darkhat ne ro ro kar yun shikayat
Kari,
Mai raton me yun to tadapta raha.
Khaamosh Raha Mene kuch na kaha,
Khud ko Ilzaam diya mai likhta
raha....

Words:

*Abr- Clouds
*Ashq- Tears
*Shabnam- dew
*Darakhat- Tree
*Gul- Flower

Nahi Aata

Mai naraaz hun tumse,
Ye kehna nahi aata.
Kisi jaandaar ka dil dukhana,
Ye bhi nahi aata.
Kisi k aitbaar ko todna,
Ye bhi nahi aata.
Dod mai agar koi gir jaaye,
Uske aage dodna phir mujhko nahi
aata.
Likh to bohot kuch sakti hun magar,
Kisi k saamne bolna, mujhko nahi
aata.
Tujhe dekhne ki ek chaah hai magar,
Tujhe dekhne ka koi bahana dil ko
nahi aata.
Dil to tuta hua h bohot,
Magar kise btain,
Kisi ko jodna nahi aata.
Ye dil ki kahani aur aankhon ka
paani,

Har kisi k samjh nahi aata.
Bas bnd krte hain kalam apna,
Kyunki zyaada likhna hamko nahi aata.

HINDUSTAN
ELIF SHAFAK
The Forty Rules of Love

Hindustan

Yeh Dharti ka tukda nahi,
Yeh hamari pehchaan hai.
Anekta mai ekta,
Yeh hamari shaan hai.
Nav'vadhu k teeke jesa,
Pyaara HINDUSTAN hai.
Bharat to Jan'ni hai sabki,
Ham iski santaan hai.
Ham par hamla soch k karna,
Kyunki ham veer jawan hai.
Desh ye sambhlega kese,
Yeh bohot aasaan hai.
Desh ko saaf va swachh rakhna,
Ye nahi ehsaan hai.

Ek Aas

Ghaltiyan tum khud hi karte ho,

Apne girehbaan mai jhank kr to dekho.

Are tum pahad bhi tod doge,

Dil ki gehraiyon ko bhaanp kr to dekho.

Kehte hain, khojo to khuda bhi milta hai,

Mehant krne vaale ko anjaam bhi milta hai.

Chiti ko bhi aakhir mehnat kerni aati hai,

Gir kar chadhna, chadh kar girna

Sabko yeh sikhlaati hai.

Mat samjho tum haar gaye, jo duniya k bhi paar gaye.

Vo duniya bhar mai zinda hain,

Naam abhi bhi zinda hain.

Mana mushkil samay hai ab,

Dilo mai sabke bhay (भय) *hai ab.*

Mat samjho k mar jayenge,

Socho k kuch kar jayenge.

Dil mai ek aas hai,

Aankhon mai ek pyas hai.

Kuch kar guzrun.

Kuch kar guzrun.

www.ingramcontent.com/pod-product-compliance
Lightning Source LLC
LaVergne TN
LVHW021307160826
845679LV00001B/247

* 9 7 9 8 8 9 5 8 8 5 7 2 7 *